If It's the Most Wonderful Time of the Year, Why Do I Feel Sad?!?

If It's the Most Wonderful Time of the Year, Why Do I Feel Sad?!?

If It's the Most Wonderful Time of the Year, Why Do I Feel Sad?!?

If It's the Most Wonderful Time of the Year, Why Do I Feel Sad?!?

If It's the Most Wonderful Time of the Year, Why Do I Feel Sad?!?

by

Michelle Dantrell

If It's the Most Wonderful Time of the Year, Why Do I Feel Sad?!?

If It's the Most Wonderful Time of the Year,
Why Do I Feel Sad?!?

DISCLAIMER:

The information provided in this book, titled "If It's the Most Wonderful Time of the Year, Why Do I Feel Sad?!?" is intended for general informational purposes only. It is important to note that the content presented in this book is not authored by mental health professionals, and therefore, should not be interpreted as professional advice or a substitute for professional guidance.

The author of this book has made reasonable efforts to ensure the accuracy and reliability of the information presented. However, mental health is a complex and evolving field, and the content provided may not encompass the entirety of available knowledge or best practices.

Readers are strongly encouraged to consult with qualified mental health physicians and practitioners regarding their specific circumstances or concerns. The information in this book should not be used as a basis for making personal decisions related to mental health treatment, medication, or therapy.

By reading this book, you acknowledge that you understand and accept the limitations of the information provided and agree to hold the author and publisher harmless from any and all claims, liabilities, or damages arising from your use of the information herein contained. Remember that your mental health is of utmost importance, and seeking professional help is strongly recommended for accurate assessment, diagnosis, and treatment.

If It's the Most Wonderful Time of the Year, Why Do I Feel Sad?!?

Hello Friends,

For as long as I can remember, I have always been sad during the holidays. Even as a child, there are pictures of me pouting. While it is somewhat surprising that any pictures were taken of me at all (which is another story all its own), the fact is, proof exists. Thinking back, I would normally have a "stomach ache" and wouldn't feel well right around Christmas day. Now, I can obviously identify the emotional issues that were troubling me at that time, only to recognize it still happens **every, single, year.**

I experience sadness during the holidays. From being a child, to getting married, to having children of my own, to them now being grown and married, EVERY stage of my life during the holidays brings a level of sadness and depression. Whether I'm solidly okay financially or I'm maxed out; in the wintery north or sunshine in the south; seeing loved ones or spending time alone; **every, single, year.**

If It's the Most Wonderful Time of the Year, Why Do I Feel Sad?!?

As with my prior books, **"Breaking the Silence: A Guide to Understanding Mental Health Issues,"** and **"WHY IS MY MOM SAD - A Guide to Helping Kids Understand Parents With Depression,"** I want this book to convey the message that YOU ARE NOT ALONE. There is nothing wrong with you, per se', in that you <u>feel</u> this way. We ALL deserve happiness and peace in our hearts and minds, not just during the holidays, but always.

Let's face it, my end game is to be your **Mental Health Hype Girl!** I want to start the conversations that end stigma and discrimination against those of us struggling with mental health issues so that society as a whole recognizes that Mental Health Is Health.

So let's get to it, and delve into the issues surrounding the holiday season sadness, triggers, and some tips for self-care. If I can contribute to making your holidays even a fraction better this year, well, Santa must have put me on his Nice List after all! I'm go glad you're here.

Let's try to enjoy the holidays together!

Michelle Dantrell
Author & Mental Health Advocate

If It's the Most Wonderful Time of the Year, Why Do I Feel Sad?!?

If It's the Most Wonderful Time of the Year, Why Do I Feel Sad?!?

Table of Contents

If It's the Most Wonderful Time of the Year, Why Do I Feel Sad?!?

If It's the Most Wonderful Time of the Year, Why Do I Feel Sad?!?

If It's the Most Wonderful Time of the Year, Why Do I Feel Sad?!?

If It's the Most Wonderful Time of the Year, Why Do I Feel Sad?!?

Chapter 1:

Understanding the Holiday Season Expectations

If It's the Most Wonderful Time of the Year, Why Do I Feel Sad?!?

If It's the Most Wonderful Time of the Year, Why Do I Feel Sad?!?

Chapter 1: Understanding the Holiday Season Expectations

The Myth of Holiday Happiness

As the holiday season approaches, there is often an air of excitement and anticipation in the air. Families come together, friends plan parties and exchange gifts, and there is an overall sense of joy and merriment. However, for those of us who struggle with depression, the holiday season can be an incredibly challenging time. In this book, "If It's the Most Wonderful Time of the Year, Why Am I Sad?!?" we aim to shed light on the reality of depression during the holidays and provide support and understanding for those who may be experiencing it.

The holiday season is often portrayed as a time of joy, happiness, and togetherness, but this can create a stark contrast for individuals living with depression. This time of year can bring about feelings of sadness, loneliness, and even guilt. In a society that places immense pressure on

everyone to be merry and bright during the holidays, those of us who are depressed can feel even more isolated and misunderstood.

It is crucial to recognize and challenge the myth of holiday happiness. The expectation that everyone should be happy during this season is unrealistic and unfair. Depression is a complex mental health condition that cannot be magically cured by twinkling lights, cookies, and festive decorations. Understanding and accepting this truth is the first step towards embracing your emotions during the holiday season.

Depression is not a choice, nor is it a reflection of your character or worth. Depression, or any mental health illness for that matter, is no more a choice than is heart disease, diabetes or pancreatitis. Depression is a <u>medical condition</u>. Therefore, it is essential to remember that your feelings of sadness or lack of holiday cheer are valid and should not be dismissed or invalidated by societal pressures.

Instead of striving to meet society's unrealistic expectations, it is important to focus on self-care and self-compassion during the holiday season. Allow yourself to feel and acknowledge your emotions **without judgment.** Surround yourself with a support system that understands and respects your journey, whether it be through therapy, friends, or online communities.

It is also important to set boundaries and prioritize your well-being. You do not have to attend every holiday gathering or participate in activities that drain your energy. Remember it is okay to say no and take time for yourself. Please let this sink in, **you do not have to attend every holiday**

gathering or social activity that drains your energy. Engage in activities that you enjoy, whether that be reading a book, watching a movie, taking a walk, spending time with pets, volunteering, or any number of activities. Simply put, do the things that will bring you joy, comfort and inner peace.

The holiday season can be particularly challenging for those of us with depression, and reaching out to a therapist or counselor can provide the necessary guidance and support, They can try to help you navigate your emotions, develop coping strategies, and find a sense of balance during this time.

Remember, you are not alone in experiencing depression during the holiday season. By acknowledging the myth of holiday happiness and embracing your emotions, you are taking an important step towards self-acceptance and well-being. Allow yourself to be gentle, kind, and patient with yourself as you navigate the complexities of this season. You afford these acts of kindness to perfect strangers, why not to yourself?

Societal Pressure to Be Happy

The stereotypical portrayal of the holidays bombards us with images of smiling faces, cozy gatherings, and **seemingly** perfect lives. However, for many people, the reality is far from the cheerful facade we are expected to display. If you find yourself feeling depressed during the holidays, you are not alone.

One of the biggest challenges faced by individuals experiencing depression during this time of year is the societal pressure to be happy. It can feel overwhelming when everyone around you seems to be filled with holiday cheer, while you struggle to find any sense of joy or enthusiasm. The pressure to put on a happy face and participate in festivities can be suffocating, leaving you feeling even more isolated and disconnected.

It is crucial to remember that your feelings are valid and that it is okay not to be happy during the holidays. **Society's expectation for constant happiness is unrealistic and can be detrimental to** your mental health. Acknowledging and accepting your emotions is the first step towards healing and finding peace within yourself.

Addressing the pressure to be happy during the holiday season while experiencing depression requires self-compassion and understanding. It is essential to prioritize your mental well-being and give yourself permission to feel whatever emotions arise. Remember that it is okay to decline invitations or take breaks from socializing if it feels overwhelming. Taking care of yourself should be your top priority.

Finding support from loved ones who understand and validate your feelings can also be immensely helpful. Reach out to trusted friends or family members who will be understanding and offer a listening ear. Connecting with others who are experiencing similar struggles can provide a sense of belonging and remind you that you are not alone in your journey.

Additionally, seeking professional help from a therapist or counselor can provide valuable guidance and support during this challenging time. They can help you navigate your emotions, develop coping strategies, and provide a safe space for you to express your feelings without judgment.

Remember, everyone experiences the holiday season differently, and it is okay to feel sad or depressed during this time. By acknowledging and addressing the societal pressure to be happy, you can begin to embrace your emotions and find peace within yourself. The path to healing starts with accepting and validating your feelings, and by doing so, you are taking a significant step towards reclaiming your holiday season and your overall well-being.

Impact of Depression on Holiday Experience

Society often expects everyone to be merry and bright during the holiday season, which can create immense pressure on individuals who are already grappling with depression. It is crucial to recognize that depression is not a choice or a reflection of one's character. By acknowledging and accepting your emotions, you can begin to navigate the holiday season in a way that is authentic to you.

Feelings of Loneliness and Isolation:

The holiday season is often portrayed as a time of joy, togetherness, and celebration. However, for many individuals *who* are battling depression, this time of year can be incredibly challenging. While others are eagerly anticipating the festivities, those struggling with depression often find themselves overwhelmed by feelings of sadness, loneliness, and a sense of disconnection from the world around them. Let's shed light on the impact of depression on the holiday experience and provide support for individuals who feel pressured to be happy despite their emotional struggles.

Depression during the holidays can intensify feelings of loneliness and isolation. While it may seem as though everyone is surrounded by loved ones and experiencing joy, it is important to remember that appearances can be deceiving.

Many people face similar struggles, and reaching out for support can make a significant difference. Seek solace in support groups, online communities, or trusted friends and family who can provide a listening ear during this time.

Managing Expectations & Self-Care:

During the holiday season, it is essential to prioritize your well-being and practice self-care. Set realistic expectations for yourself and avoid comparing your experience to that of others. Understand that it is okay to decline invitations or take breaks when needed. Engaging in activities that bring you comfort and peace, such as practicing mindfulness, engaging in creative outlets, or spending time in nature, can help alleviate the impact of depression on your holiday experience.

Seeking Professional Help:

If depression is severely impacting your ability to enjoy the holiday season, or if you are struggling with thoughts of hurting yourself or others, it is vital to reach out to a mental health professional immediately. Therapists and counselors can provide valuable guidance, support, and coping strategies to help you navigate the challenges of depression during the holidays. Of course if you are in imminent danger, contact 9-1-1 immediately.

Depression during the holiday season can make it feel as though you are alone in your struggles. However, it is important to remember that you are not alone, and there is support available. By acknowledging the impact of depression on your holiday experience and embracing your emotions, you can begin to find ways to navigate this time of year authentically. Remember to prioritize self-care, seek support from trusted individuals, and reach out to professionals if needed. It is possible to find moments of joy and connection, even amidst the darkness of depression.

Chapter 2:

Unveiling the Reality of Depression During the Holidays

Chapter 2: Unveiling the Reality of Depression During the Holidays

Defining Depression

Depression is an emotional state that affects millions of people worldwide, and the holiday season is no exception. While society expects us to be merry and joyful during this time, many individuals find themselves struggling with feelings of sadness, loneliness, and despair. We will now delve into the true definition of depression and how it relates to the pressure society imposes on us to be happy during the holiday season.

Depression is not simply feeling down or having the "holiday blues." It is a complex mental health condition that goes beyond temporary sadness. It is characterized by persistent feelings of emptiness, hopelessness, and a general lack of interest or pleasure in activities that were once enjoyable. Depressed individuals often experience changes in appetite, sleep patterns, and concentration, making it difficult to function in daily life.

During the holiday season, the contrast between societal expectations and one's own emotional state can be particularly challenging. The pressure to be happy and celebrate can intensify feelings of guilt and shame for those experiencing depression. It is important to remember that depression is not a choice, nor is it a reflection of personal failure. It is a medical condition that requires understanding, empathy, and support.

Addressing the pressure to be happy during the holiday season while experiencing depression starts with acknowledging and accepting your emotions. It is crucial to recognize that your feelings are valid and deserving of attention. Suppressing or denying these emotions will only exacerbate the internal struggle.

Next, it is essential to communicate your emotions with loved ones and seek support. Reach out to trusted friends or family members who can provide a listening ear and a non-judgmental space. It is vital to surround yourself with individuals who understand that happiness is not a requirement during the holidays and who are willing to support you unconditionally.

Additionally, seeking professional help is crucial in managing depression during this time. Therapists and counselors can provide effective coping strategies, such as cognitive-behavioral therapy, medication, or other evidence-based treatments tailored to your specific needs.

Remember, it is okay not to be okay during the holiday season. Embracing your emotions and seeking support will help you navigate this challenging time and find moments of peace and solace amidst the holiday frenzy. By acknowledging the pressure to be happy and addressing it head-on, you are taking an important step towards embracing your emotions and finding healing, both during the holiday season and beyond.

The purpose of "If It's the Most Wonderful Time of the Year, Why Do I Feel Sad?!?" is to VALIDATE your feelings of depression. We are each responsible for owning our TRUTH and you have come to a place of understanding and support in your personal journey.

Symptoms of Depression

One of the most common symptoms of depression during the holiday season is a persistent feeling of sadness or emptiness. You may find it difficult to muster up any genuine excitement or joy, despite the festive atmosphere surrounding you. This feeling of sadness can be accompanied by a loss of interest or pleasure in activities that you once enjoyed, including holiday traditions or spending time with loved ones.

Another symptom to be aware of is a significant change in appetite or weight. Depression can often lead to a loss of appetite, resulting in unintended weight loss. On the other hand (which is MY hand), some individuals may turn to food as a source of comfort, resulting in weight gain. These changes in eating habits can further contribute to feelings of guilt or self-esteem issues, exacerbating the symptoms of depression.

Sleep disturbances are also common during the holiday season for those experiencing depression. You may find it difficult to fall asleep or stay asleep, leading to feelings of fatigue and exhaustion. Conversely, some individuals may find themselves sleeping excessively as a means of escaping from the emotional pain they are experiencing.

Feelings of worthlessness or excessive guilt are additional symptoms that can be particularly challenging during the holiday season. You may compare yourself to others and feel inadequate for not being able to experience the same level of happiness and excitement. These negative thoughts can further perpetuate the cycle of depression and make it even more difficult to reach out for support.

It is important to remember that depression is a real and valid condition, and it does not discriminate based on the time of year. If you are experiencing any of these symptoms during the holiday season, it is crucial to seek help and support. Reach out to a trusted friend, family member, or mental health professional who can provide you with the guidance and assistance you need.

Remember, you are not alone, and it is okay to prioritize your mental health during the holiday season. By acknowledging and addressing the pressure to be happy, you can begin to embrace your emotions and find ways to navigate through this challenging time.

Unique Challenges Faced by Depressed Individuals during the Holidays

The holiday season is often portrayed as a time of joy, celebration, and togetherness. However, for those struggling with depression, this time of year can be particularly challenging. While everyone around seems to be filled with happiness and excitement, individuals battling depression often experience a stark contrast in their emotions. Let's explore the unique challenges faced by depressed individuals during the holidays, with a focus on addressing the pressure to be happy while experiencing depression.

One of the main challenges individuals with depression face during the holidays is the societal expectation to be joyful and merry. There is an immense pressure to put on a facade of happiness, as friends, family, and even society at large, believe that this time of year should be nothing but blissful. However, for those struggling with depression, it is not as simple as just "being happy." This pressure to conform to the expectations can exacerbate feelings of guilt and shame, leaving individuals feeling isolated and misunderstood.

Another significant challenge faced by depressed individuals during the holidays is the constant reminder of their own emotional struggles. The emphasis on family, love, and connection can intensify feelings of loneliness and isolation for those who may not have a strong support system.

This time of year is a specific reminder of personal loss of loved ones.   Whether is be through distance, divorce, or death, the holidays exacerbate our feelings of personal loss.

Additionally, the overwhelming commercialization of the holidays can create a sense of inadequacy, as individuals may compare their own lives to the seemingly perfect ones portrayed in advertisements and social media.

Moreover, the holiday season often disrupts routines and introduces additional stressors, which can further exacerbate depressive symptoms. The financial strain of gift-giving, the pressure to attend social events, and the expectation to meet societal standards of perfection can all contribute to increased stress and anxiety. These added stressors can make it even more challenging for depressed individuals to cope with their emotions effectively.

In order to address these unique challenges, it is crucial to prioritize self-care during the holiday season. This means setting realistic expectations for yourself and allowing yourself to experience a range of emotions, including sadness or grief. It is essential to communicate your feelings to trusted loved ones and seek support from mental health professionals if needed. Additionally, we need to be proactive in finding alternative ways to engage in holiday activities that align with your own needs and preferences can help alleviate some of the pressure to conform.

Remember, your emotions are valid, and it is okay to feel depressed during the holidays when everyone expects you to be happy. By acknowledging and embracing your emotions, you can navigate this season with greater self-compassion and find moments of joy and peace amidst the challenges.

If It's the Most Wonderful Time of the Year, Why Do I Feel Sad?!?

Chapter 3:

Navigating the Emotional Rollercoaster

Chapter 3: Navigating the Emotional Rollercoaster

Acknowledging and Validating Emotions

The holiday season is often portrayed as a time of joy, celebration, and togetherness. However, for many individuals, this time of year can bring about intense feelings of sadness, loneliness, and depression. It is crucial to recognize and validate these emotions, as they are just as valid and important as the feelings of happiness that are often expected during this season.

When everyone around you seems to be caught up in the holiday spirit, it can be incredibly challenging to acknowledge and accept your own feelings of depression. Society often places immense pressure on individuals to conform to the idea that they should be happy during this time. However, it is vital to remember that your emotions are valid, and it is okay to not feel the same level of joy as those around you.

Acknowledging your emotions is the first step towards healing and finding peace during the holiday season. By allowing yourself to feel the sadness, loneliness, or depression, you are giving yourself permission to experience your emotions fully. It is important to remember that emotions are a natural part of being human and that it is okay to not be okay during this time.

Validating your emotions means recognizing that they are real and legitimate. It is common for individuals experiencing depression during the holidays to dismiss their feelings, thinking that they are irrational or that they should just "snap out of it." However, this self-judgment only exacerbates the negative emotions and can make it even more challenging to cope.

Instead, practice self-compassion and remind yourself that it is okay to feel the way you do. Surround yourself with a support system of understanding and empathetic individuals who can validate your emotions. Engage in self-care activities that bring you comfort and solace, such as journaling, exercising, or spending time in nature.

Remember, it is essential to prioritize your mental health and well-being during the holiday season. By acknowledging and validating your emotions, you are taking a significant step towards embracing your true self and finding peace amidst the holiday chaos. Allow yourself to feel, to heal, and to navigate this season at your own pace. You are not alone, and your feelings matter.

Coping Mechanisms for Emotional Turmoil

Addressing the pressure to be happy during the holiday season while experiencing depression is essential for implementing your coping mechanisms.

1. **Validate your feelings**: It is crucial to acknowledge and honor your emotions, even if they do not align with society's expectations. Understand that it is okay to feel sad, lonely, or overwhelmed during this time. Give yourself permission to experience your emotions without judgment.

2. **Seek support**: Reach out to trusted friends or family members who can provide a supportive ear. Opening up about your struggles can help alleviate feelings of loneliness and isolation. Additionally, consider seeking professional help from a therapist or counselor who specializes in depression. They can provide guidance and tools to manage your emotions during the holiday season.

3. **Practice self-care**: Take time for yourself and prioritize self-care activities. Engage in activities that bring you joy and provide a sense of calm. This could include reading a book, taking walks in nature, practicing mindfulness or meditation, or pursuing creative outlets such as painting or writing.

4. **Set realistic expectations**: Avoid putting pressure on yourself to meet societal expectations of holiday cheer. Understand that it is okay to set boundaries and say no to certain obligations or events if they are too overwhelming. Focus on what feels manageable and meaningful to you, rather than trying to meet external expectations.

5. **Connect with others who understand**: Seek out support groups or online communities where you can connect with others who are experiencing similar feelings during the holiday season. Sharing your struggles with individuals who understand can provide a sense of validation and camaraderie. Depression can be VERY lonely, and there is nothing better than having someone that truly understands you and is not judgmental.

Remember, it is essential to prioritize your mental health and well-being during this time. Embracing your emotions and finding healthy coping mechanisms will allow you to navigate the holiday season with self-compassion and strength. You are not alone, and there is hope for finding moments of peace and joy amidst the emotional turmoil.

Seeking Support and Building a Support Network

Addressing the pressure to be happy during the holiday season while experiencing depression can be an overwhelming and isolating experience. The expectations society places on us to be joyful and festive can intensify feelings of sadness, making it even more challenging to reach out for help. However, seeking support and building a support network during this time can be crucial in navigating through the holiday season.

Firstly, it's important to acknowledge that it is okay to feel down during the holidays. Many people experience depression during this time, and it's essential to remind yourself that your emotions are valid. By accepting your feelings and being kind to yourself, you can begin to take the necessary steps towards seeking support.

One way to seek support is by reaching out to trusted friends or family members. Share your struggles with someone you feel comfortable with and let them know what you're going through. Opening up about your depression can help alleviate the burden of pretending to be happy and allow others to understand your situation. Remember, true friends and loved ones will offer their support and understanding.

In addition to personal connections, there are various support networks available both online and in-person. Consider joining support groups or forums specifically tailored to individuals experiencing depression during the holidays. These communities can provide a safe space to share your feelings, offer advice, and connect with others who are going through similar challenges. Online platforms, such as social media groups or forums, can also provide a sense of belonging and understanding.

Professional help is another valuable resource when dealing with depression during the holiday season. Seek assistance from therapists, counselors, or psychologists who specialize in mental health. These professionals can provide guidance, offer coping strategies, and help you navigate through the emotional turmoil that the holiday season may bring.

Lastly, remember to take care of yourself. Engage in self-care activities that bring you comfort and joy, whether it's taking a long bath, practicing mindfulness, or engaging in a hobby you enjoy. Allow yourself to set boundaries and prioritize your well-being over societal expectations.

If It's the Most Wonderful Time of the Year,
Why Do I Feel Sad?!?

Addressing the pressure to be happy during the holiday season while experiencing depression can be challenging, but seeking support and building a support network can make a significant difference. Reach out to trusted friends and family, join supportive communities, seek professional help, and prioritize self-care. Remember, it's okay to feel the way you do, and by seeking support, you can navigate through the holiday season with more understanding, compassion, and resilience.

Chapter 4:

Challenging the Stigma and Misconceptions

Chapter 4: Challenging the Stigma and Misconceptions

Addressing the Stigma Surrounding Depression

The holiday season is often dubbed as the most wonderful time of the year, filled with joy, love, and laughter. However, for many individuals who are battling depression, it can be an incredibly challenging and lonely period. The pressure to be happy and full of holiday spirit can exacerbate feelings of sadness and isolation, leading to a deep sense of guilt and shame. Let's delve into the stigma surrounding depression during the holidays and discuss strategies to address this pressure and embrace your emotions authentically.

It is important to acknowledge that depression is a real and valid mental health condition that can affect anyone, regardless of the season. However, during the holiday season, society's expectations of constant happiness can intensify the stigma surrounding depression. People may struggle to understand how someone can be depressed when everyone around them seems to be brimming with joy. This misunderstanding can lead to feelings of inadequacy, further isolating individuals who are already battling with their own internal demons.

As a person struggling with with mental health issues, specifically depression and anxiety, I can attest to the fact that it is completely disheartening to when these issues are trivialized and we're made to feel as though these illnesses are a choice.

The first step in addressing this stigma is to recognize that your feelings are valid and that you are not alone. It is crucial to remind yourself that depression does not discriminate, and experiencing it during the holiday season does not make you any less deserving of support and understanding. Surround yourself with a trusted support system, whether it be friends, family, or mental health professionals who can provide a safe space for you to express your emotions without judgment.

If you cannot find support from those close to you, consider reassessing the amount of time you spend with those people during your bouts of depression.

Embracing your emotions authentically means allowing yourself to feel whatever you need to feel. If that means experiencing moments of sadness or grief during the holiday season, it is perfectly normal. Remember, there is no right or wrong way to feel during this time. Instead of forcing yourself to conform to societal expectations, give yourself permission to prioritize your mental health and well-being. Set realistic expectations, and don't feel obligated to engage in activities that may trigger or worsen your depression.

Educating those around you about depression can also help combat the stigma. Open up to your loved ones about your struggles and provide them with resources (such as this book, lol) to better understand depression. By sharing your experiences, you not only allow yourself to be vulnerable, but you also contribute to a larger conversation about mental health, ultimately breaking down the stigma and fostering a more supportive environment.

Addressing the pressure to be happy during the holiday season while experiencing depression requires self-compassion, understanding, and a supportive network. By acknowledging the stigma surrounding depression, embracing your emotions authentically, and educating others about this mental health condition, you can navigate the holiday season with greater self-acceptance and resilience. Remember, your well-being should always be your top priority, regardless of societal expectations.

Educating Others about the Realities of Depression during the Holidays

As we have repeated the expectations of society upon those of us struggling with depression (again, or ANY other mental health illness) we will address the pressure to be happy during the holiday season while experiencing depression, and educate others about the realities of this mental health condition.

Depression is an invisible illness that often goes unnoticed, especially during the festive season. People who are depressed may put on a façade, pretending to be happy and participating in holiday activities to avoid judgment or questions from others. It is crucial to educate those around us about the mask of depression, helping them understand that someone may be battling their own demons beneath the festive exterior.

One of the most significant ways we can support those who are depressed during the holidays is by fostering empathy. Educating others about depression can lead to a greater understanding of the challenges faced by individuals in this situation. By explaining the symptoms, such as persistent sadness, loss of interest, and fatigue, we can help others grasp the complexities of this mental health condition.

When someone confides in us about their depression during the holiday season, it is essential to create a safe space for them to express their emotions. Educate others about the importance of active listening, validation, and avoiding judgment. This understanding and acceptance can go a long way in providing comfort and support to those who need it most.

While the holiday season can be overwhelming, there are alternative ways to support individuals battling depression during this time. By educating others about the various resources available, such as therapy, support groups, and helplines, we can ensure that individuals receive the help they need. Encouraging open conversations about mental health and reducing the stigma can also contribute to a more supportive environment.

Depression during the holiday season is a reality for many individuals, even though it may contradict societal expectations of happiness. By educating others about this struggle, we can create a more compassionate and understanding society. Let us embrace empathy, foster safe spaces for open conversations, and provide alternative support, ensuring that no one feels alone in their battle against depression during the holidays.

Promoting Empathy and Understanding

Addressing the pressure to be happy during the holiday season while experiencing depression. The holiday season is often depicted as a time of joy, warmth, and togetherness. However, for many individuals struggling with depression, it can be an overwhelming and challenging period. While others are celebrating and spreading cheer, those suffering from depression often find themselves feeling isolated and misunderstood.

This subtopic aims to promote empathy and understanding for those who experience depression during the holidays, shedding light on their internal struggles and offering guidance for both individuals facing depression and their loved ones.

It is crucial to acknowledge that depression is not a choice, and it cannot be easily overcome with a change in attitude or a festive environment. Depression is a complex mental health condition that affects millions of people worldwide, and the holiday season can intensify these feelings of sadness and isolation. It is essential for society to recognize that not everyone experiences the holiday season in the same way and that it is okay to feel differently during this time.

For individuals experiencing depression during the holidays, it is essential to prioritize self-care and reach out for support. Let's look at offers for practical strategies for self-care, such as engaging in activities that bring comfort, setting realistic expectations, and seeking professional help when needed. It also provides guidance for loved ones on how to offer support and understanding to those facing depression, emphasizing the importance of active listening, empathy, and avoiding judgment.

Additionally, it is necessary to open communication and set boundaries. It encourages individuals to express their needs and concerns to their loved ones, allowing for a deeper understanding of their experiences and fostering a sense of empathy. By promoting open and honest conversations, it becomes easier for both parties to navigate the holiday season together, ensuring that everyone feels heard and respected.

Ultimately, it is crucial to create a compassionate and understanding space for those who experience depression during the holidays. It encourages society to move beyond the facade of happiness and embrace the diversity of emotions that can arise during this time. By promoting empathy and understanding, we can foster a more inclusive and supportive environment for all, allowing individuals facing depression to find solace and strength in their journey.

Chapter 5:

Embracing Self-Care and Self-Compassion

If It's the Most Wonderful Time of the Year,
Why Do I Feel Sad?!?

Chapter 5: Embracing Self-Care and Self-Compassion

Self-Care Strategies during the Holiday Season

Addressing the pressure to be happy during the holiday season while experiencing depression can be incredibly challenging. Society often portrays this time as one filled with joy, cheer, and celebration. However, for many individuals, it can be a stark reminder of their own struggles and feelings of isolation. If you find yourself in this situation, it is important to prioritize self-care and implement strategies to navigate this difficult period effectively.

First and foremost, it is crucial to acknowledge and accept your emotions. It is okay to not feel happy during the holidays. Give yourself permission to feel whatever emotions arise and understand that it is a normal part of your journey. Allow yourself to grieve, acknowledge your pain, and be gentle with yourself.

Find support in your loved ones. Reach out to trusted friends or family members who can provide a listening ear or a comforting presence. Communicate your feelings honestly and let them know that you may need some extra support during this time. Surrounding yourself with understanding and empathetic individuals can make a significant difference in how you navigate the holiday season.

Engage in self-care activities that bring you comfort and peace. This may include spending time in nature, practicing prayer or meditation, engaging in creative outlets such as painting or writing, or simply taking a warm bath. Prioritize activities that nourish your soul and provide moments of respite amidst the holiday chaos.

Set boundaries and say no when necessary. It is important to recognize your limits and not overextend yourself during this time. Understand that it is okay to decline invitations or opt-out of certain events if they contribute to your feelings of stress or overwhelm. Prioritize your well-being above societal expectations.

Consider seeking professional help. If your depression intensifies during the holiday season, it may be helpful to consult a therapist or counselor who specializes in mental health. They can provide valuable guidance, support, and coping strategies tailored to your specific needs.

Remember, the holiday season does not define your worth or happiness. Embrace the fact that everyone experiences the holidays differently, and it is okay to prioritize your mental health above all else. Be kind to yourself, practice self-compassion, and remember that brighter days will come. You are not alone in your journey, and there is hope for a brighter future beyond the facade of the holiday season.

Developing a Personalized Self-Care Routine

The holiday season is often portrayed as a time of joy, laughter, and celebration. But for many individuals, it can be a challenging period, especially if they are experiencing depression during this time. While the world around you may seem to expect happiness, it is essential to acknowledge and honor your emotions. Let's explore the concept of developing a personalized self-care routine to help navigate through the holidays and embrace your emotions authentically.

1. **Recognize Your Feelings**: It is perfectly normal to feel depressed or down during the holiday season, even if society expects you to be happy. Acknowledge your feelings and remember that it is okay to experience a range of emotions.

2. **Prioritize Self-Care**: Developing a personalized self-care routine is crucial during this time. Identify activities that bring you comfort and joy, such as engaging in hobbies, reading a book, going for walks, practicing mindfulness, or spending time with loved ones who understand and support you.

3. **Set Boundaries**: Don't be afraid to set boundaries with others. If certain social gatherings or events trigger your depression, it's okay to decline invitations or limit your participation. Focus on what feels right for you and prioritize your mental well-being.

4. **Seek Support**: Reach out to trusted friends, family members, or professionals who can provide support during this challenging period. Surrounding yourself with compassionate individuals who understand your struggles can make a significant difference in your journey.

5. **Practice Gratitude**: While it may be difficult, try to cultivate a sense of gratitude for the positives in your life. Start a gratitude journal, where you can write down a few things you are grateful for each day. This practice can help shift your focus from negative thoughts to the positive aspects of your life.

6. **Engage in Physical Activity**: Exercise has been proven to boost mood and alleviate symptoms of depression. Incorporate regular physical activity into your routine, whether it's going for a walk, practicing yoga, or engaging in any form of movement that you enjoy.

7. **Create Meaningful Traditions**: Instead of conforming to societal expectations, create your own meaningful traditions that align with your values and bring you joy. It could be volunteering, participating in a creative project, or engaging in activities that give you a sense of purpose.

Remember, it's okay to prioritize yourself and your mental well-being during the holiday season. By developing a personalized self-care routine, you can navigate through this period with authenticity, embracing your emotions and finding moments of joy and peace amidst the holiday chaos.

Practicing Self-Compassion to Combat Negative Self-Talk

The holiday season is often portrayed as a time of joy, love, and celebration. However, for many individuals struggling with depression, this time of year can be incredibly challenging. The pressure to be happy and cheerful when you are feeling anything but can intensify feelings of sadness, loneliness, and isolation. It's important to remember that your experiences and emotions are valid, and you are not alone in feeling this way.

One powerful tool that can help combat negative self-talk during the holiday season is practicing self-compassion. Self-compassion involves treating yourself with kindness, understanding, and acceptance, especially during difficult times. It is about acknowledging your pain and suffering, while also offering yourself the same level of care and compassion you would give to a loved one.

When depression weighs heavily on your shoulders, it's easy to fall into a cycle of negative self-talk. You might find yourself engaging in self-critical thoughts, believing that you should be happy like everyone else. However, it's important to challenge these thoughts and remind yourself that depression is an illness, not a choice. By practicing self-compassion, you can start to break free from the unrealistic expectations placed upon you during the holiday season.

Begin by acknowledging your emotions without judgment. Recognize that it is okay to feel sad, lonely, or overwhelmed, even when everyone around you seems to be filled with holiday cheer. Allow yourself to grieve for the emotions you wish you were experiencing, while also offering yourself comfort and understanding.

Next, practice self-care. Engage in activities that bring you joy, comfort, or peace, even if they may be different from traditional holiday activities. Perhaps you find solace in reading a book, taking long walks in nature, or listening to calming music. Whatever it may be, prioritize your well-being and engage in activities that nourish your soul.

Additionally, reach out for support. Talk to a trusted friend, family member, or therapist who can provide a listening ear and offer guidance. Remember, you don't have to face depression alone, especially during the holiday season.

Lastly, be gentle with yourself. Give yourself permission to take a step back from the pressure and expectations that surround this time of year. Set realistic goals and boundaries for yourself, and remember that it's okay to say no to activities or events that may be too overwhelming.

Practicing self-compassion during the holiday season can help alleviate the burden of negative self-talk and allow you to embrace your emotions in a healthy and loving way. **Remember, your worth is not determined by your ability to put on a happy face, but by your resilience and willingness to care for yourself.**

Chapter 6:

Setting Boundaries and Managing Expectations

If It's the Most Wonderful Time of the Year,
Why Do I Feel Sad?!?

Chapter 6: Setting Boundaries and Managing Expectations

Recognizing Personal Limitations

The holiday season, often hailed as a time of joy and cheer, can be a challenging period for many individuals. While society expects us to be happy and festive during this time, there are those among us who battle with depression and find it difficult to meet these expectations. If you are one of those people who feel weighed down by the pressure to be happy during the holiday season, it is crucial to recognize and acknowledge your personal limitations.

First and foremost, it is important to understand that your feelings are valid. Depression is a complex and multifaceted condition that can affect anyone, regardless of the time of year. The holiday season may intensify these emotions, but does not diminish the validity of what you are experiencing. It is essential to give yourself permission to feel sad or overwhelmed, without guilt or judgment.

Recognizing your personal limitations means understanding that you may not be able to participate in all the activities or social gatherings that are expected during this time. It is alright to decline invitations or take breaks when needed. Prioritize self-care and focus on activities that bring you comfort and peace. Whether it's going for a walk, reading a book, or spending time with a trusted friend or family member, allow yourself the space to recharge and heal.

Additionally, it is crucial to seek support from those around you. Often, people struggling with depression during the holiday season isolate themselves, feeling like they are burdening others with their emotions. However, reaching out for support is not a sign of weakness but an act of strength. Share your feelings with a trusted friend or family member who can offer a listening ear or seek professional help from a therapist or counselor. Remember, you are not alone in your struggles, and there are people who genuinely care about your well-being.

Lastly, it is important to set realistic expectations for yourself. The pressure to be happy during the holiday season can be overwhelming, but it is essential to remember that healing takes time. Be kind to yourself and focus on small victories. Celebrate the moments of joy and progress, no matter how small they may seem.

Recognizing your personal limitations during the holiday season is crucial for individuals experiencing depression. Acknowledge your feelings, prioritize self-care, seek support, and set realistic expectations. Remember, your well-being is paramount, and by embracing your emotions and honoring your limitations, you can navigate the holiday season with greater ease and self-compassion.

Communicating Boundaries with Loved Ones

The holiday season is often depicted as a time of joy, love, and celebration. But what if you find yourself feeling the exact opposite? For many individuals, the pressure to be happy during this time can feel overwhelming, especially when dealing with depression. It's essential to recognize that your emotions are valid, and it's okay not to feel the same level of excitement as everyone else. However, communicating your boundaries with loved ones can be an effective way to navigate through this challenging period.

It is crucial to understand that your loved ones may not fully comprehend the depths of your depression. They may unintentionally contribute to the pressure you feel to be happy by expecting you to participate in various activities or social gatherings. It's essential to communicate your boundaries openly and honestly. Choose a calm and private moment to talk to them, explaining that you are experiencing depression and that it may affect your ability to fully engage in holiday festivities.

Help your loved ones understand that depression is not a choice and that it cannot be simply overcome by forcing yourself to be happy. Educate them about the nature of depression, its symptoms, and its impact on your daily life. By providing them with this information, you are empowering them to support you in the most effective and understanding way possible.

Additionally, be specific about your boundaries and limitations. Let your loved ones know what you can and cannot handle during the holiday season. Perhaps you need some alone time or prefer smaller, more intimate gatherings. Make it clear that it's not a reflection of their efforts or their love for you; it's simply about taking care of yourself and respecting your emotional needs.

Remember that setting boundaries is not selfish; it's an act of self-care. By communicating your boundaries, you are prioritizing your mental health and well-being. It's essential to remember that you are not alone in your struggles, and there are people who genuinely care about your happiness and want to support you.

Communicating boundaries with loved ones during the holiday season can be challenging, especially when dealing with depression. However, it is a vital step in taking care of yourself and ensuring your mental well-being. By educating your loved ones about your depression, expressing your specific needs, and reminding them of their unconditional support, you can navigate this difficult time with more understanding and compassion. Remember, it's okay not to be happy during the holidays, and your emotions are valid.

Letting Go of Unrealistic Expectations

The holiday season is often portrayed as a time of joy, togetherness, and happiness. However, for many people who experience depression, this time of year can be particularly challenging. While others seem to be reveling in the festivities, those struggling with depression may find themselves feeling isolated, misunderstood, and overwhelmed by the pressure to be happy. It is essential to address these unrealistic expectations and learn to let go of them in order to embrace your emotions fully during the holiday season.

First and foremost, it is crucial to realize that your feelings are valid. Depression is a real and complex condition that cannot be overcome simply because it is the holiday season. It is okay to not feel joyful during this time, and it is essential to give yourself permission to feel the full range of your emotions. By acknowledging and accepting your feelings, you can begin the process of healing and self-compassion.

One of the most challenging aspects of depression during the holidays is the pressure to conform to societal expectations. Understand that you do not have to meet these expectations. Your worth is not determined by how happy or festive you appear to others. Give yourself permission to create your own holiday experience, one that aligns with your needs and preferences. This might mean setting boundaries, saying no to certain events or traditions, and prioritizing self-care.

Additionally, seek support from trusted friends, family, or mental health professionals. Reach out to those who understand and validate your emotions. Surround yourself with a support system that accepts you as you are, without judgment or pressure to be happy. You are not alone in your experiences, and connecting with others who share similar struggles can provide a sense of comfort and understanding.

Remember, the holiday season is not solely about happiness. It is about connection, reflection, and self-care. Embrace the opportunity to nurture your emotional well-being by engaging in activities that bring you a sense of peace and fulfillment. This might include journaling, practicing mindfulness, engaging in creative outlets, or seeking solace in nature.

By letting go of unrealistic expectations and embracing your emotions during the holiday season, you can navigate the challenges of depression with greater resilience and self-compassion. Remember, **it is okay to not be okay, and your worth is not defined by your ability to be happy during this time**. Give yourself permission to prioritize your mental health and well-being, and remember that healing is a journey that takes time and patience.

Chapter 7:

Finding Joy and Meaning in Non-Traditional Ways

If It's the Most Wonderful Time of the Year, Why Do I Feel Sad?!?

If It's the Most Wonderful Time of the Year, Why Do I Feel Sad?!?

Chapter 7: Finding Joy and Meaning in Non-Traditional Ways

Exploring Alternative Holiday Traditions

The holiday season is often portrayed as a time of joy, celebration, and togetherness. However, not everyone feels this way, especially those who experience depression during this time of the year. If you find yourself feeling down, overwhelmed, or disconnected from the festive spirit, it's essential to acknowledge your emotions and explore alternative holiday traditions that can help you navigate through this challenging period.

Traditional holiday celebrations can inadvertently exacerbate feelings of sadness and isolation, as societal expectations often demand constant happiness and cheerfulness. It's crucial to remember that it's okay to feel differently during this time of the year. By acknowledging your emotions, you can start finding alternative ways to honor the season while being true to yourself.

One alternative holiday tradition is to focus on self-care. Instead of trying to keep up with the hectic pace of the season, take time for yourself. Engage in activities that bring you comfort and joy, such as reading a good book, taking long walks in nature, or practicing mindfulness and meditation. By prioritizing self-care, you can create a sense of peace and balance amidst the chaos.

Another alternative is to volunteer or give back to your community. Helping others can be a powerful way to shift your focus away from your own struggles and find purpose during the holiday season. Whether it's volunteering at a local shelter, organizing a food drive, or spending time with the elderly, acts of kindness can bring a sense of fulfillment and meaning to your life.

Additionally, exploring new traditions that align with your values and interests can be liberating. Consider celebrating the holidays in a way that feels authentic to you. This could involve creating a non-traditional feast with friends, hosting a game night, or even planning a getaway to a peaceful destination. By embracing alternative traditions, you can break free from the pressure to conform and find joy in your unique way.

Remember, it's essential to communicate your feelings and needs with your loved ones. Sharing your experience of depression during the holidays can help them understand what you're going through, potentially alleviating some of the pressure you may feel. Surround yourself with a support system that embraces your emotions and supports your journey towards healing.

While the holiday season can be challenging for those experiencing depression, exploring alternative holiday traditions can provide a path towards embracing your emotions and finding peace during this time. By prioritizing self-care, giving back to your community, and creating new traditions, you can navigate through the season with authenticity and grace. Remember, you are not alone, and it's okay to feel the way you do.

Focusing on Personal Values and Meaningful Activities

The holiday season is often portrayed as a time of joy, celebration, and togetherness. However, for many people, especially those struggling with depression, this time of year can be incredibly challenging. The pressure to be happy and engage in festive activities can exacerbate feelings of sadness and isolation. If you find yourself in this situation, it's important to remember that it's okay not to feel joyful during the holidays. By focusing on your personal values and engaging in meaningful activities, you can navigate through the season with more ease and find a sense of purpose.

One way to address the pressure to be happy is by acknowledging and accepting your emotions. It's normal to experience a range of feelings, including sadness or loneliness, during the holidays. Instead of trying to force yourself to feel a certain way, give yourself permission to feel what you're feeling. Remember, your emotions are valid, and it's important to honor them.

Another helpful strategy is to identify and focus on your personal values. Ask yourself what truly matters to you during this time of year. It could be spending quality time with loved ones, giving back to your community, or practicing self-care. By aligning your activities with your values, you can create a sense of meaning and purpose, even if you're not feeling particularly joyful.

Engaging in meaningful activities can also help combat feelings of depression during the holidays. Consider volunteering at a local charity, participating in a support group, or pursuing a hobby that brings you joy. These activities can provide a sense of fulfillment and connection, helping to alleviate some of the pressure to be happy.

Remember, it's important to prioritize self-care during this time. Take care of your physical and mental well-being by getting enough rest, eating nourishing foods, and engaging in activities that bring you peace and relaxation. Don't be afraid to set boundaries and say no to activities that don't align with your values or drain your energy.

If you're experiencing depression during the holiday season, it's essential to focus on your personal values and engage in meaningful activities. By acknowledging and accepting your emotions, aligning your activities with your values, and prioritizing self-care, you can navigate through the season with more ease and find a sense of purpose. Remember, it's okay not to be happy during the holidays, and your well-being should always be the priority.

Cultivating Gratitude and Appreciation

Next, let's explore the power of gratitude and appreciation in navigating the holiday season while experiencing depression. Although it may seem counterintuitive, cultivating these positive emotions can provide solace and support during challenging times. By shifting our focus from what we lack to what we have, we can find moments of peace and contentment.

First and foremost, it is essential to acknowledge and accept your emotions. Recognize that it is perfectly normal to feel sad or lonely during the holidays, even when everyone around you seems to be radiating happiness. Allow yourself to grieve and process these emotions, knowing that it is okay to not be okay.

Once you have acknowledged your feelings, try incorporating gratitude into your daily routine. Start a gratitude journal where you can jot down three things you are grateful for each day. These can be as simple as a warm cup of tea, a kind word from a friend, or a beautiful sunset. By consciously focusing on the positive aspects of your life, you can bring a sense of appreciation and perspective.

Additionally, seek out activities that align with your interests and bring you joy. Engaging in hobbies or volunteering for a cause you are passionate about can provide a sense of purpose and fulfillment. Surround yourself with supportive individuals who understand and respect your emotions, and reach out to them when you need a listening ear or a comforting presence.

One of my favorite motivational speakers, Jon Gordon, starts each day with a gratitude walk. He suggests this as a 10-30 minute walk, speaking out loud what you are thankful for. This is surely a way to start your day on a positive note and, if we're being honest, you could never run out of things to be thankful for.

Remember, it is important to set realistic expectations for yourself during the holiday season. Instead of striving for perfection or forcing yourself to be happy, prioritize self-care and self-compassion. Allow yourself to grieve, rest, and heal at your own pace.

Cultivating gratitude and appreciation can be a powerful tool in navigating the holiday season while experiencing depression. By accepting your emotions, practicing gratitude, engaging in activities that bring you joy, and surrounding yourself with supportive individuals, you can find moments of solace and contentment amidst the pressure to be happy. Remember, it's okay to not be okay, and you are not alone in your journey.

Chapter 8:

Seeking Professional Help and Resources

If It's the Most Wonderful Time of the Year, Why Do I Feel Sad?!?

If It's the Most Wonderful Time of the Year,
Why Do I Feel Sad?!?

Chapter 8: Seeking Professional Help and Resources

The Benefits of Therapy and Counseling

Addressing the pressure to be happy during the holiday season while experiencing depression can be an overwhelming task. As the world around you seems to be immersed in joy and cheer, it's easy to feel isolated and misunderstood. However, it's important to remember that you are not alone in your struggle. Seeking therapy and counseling can offer invaluable support and guidance during this challenging time, helping you navigate through your emotions and find solace amidst the holiday chaos.

Therapy and counseling provide a safe and non-judgmental space for you to explore your feelings and concerns. A trained therapist or counselor can help you understand the root causes of your depression, offering insights into the unique challenges you face during the holiday season. By delving into your emotions, you can gain a deeper understanding of yourself and develop effective coping mechanisms to better navigate the pressure to be happy.

One of the significant benefits of therapy and counseling is the opportunity to learn and practice self-care. During the holiday season, it's crucial to prioritize your well-being and give yourself permission to feel what you truly feel. Therapists and counselors can guide you in developing strategies to set boundaries, manage expectations, and engage in activities that bring you comfort and joy. By focusing on self-care, you can alleviate some of the pressure to conform to societal expectations and embrace your own emotions authentically.

Additionally, therapy and counseling can help you build a support system. The holiday season can intensify feelings of loneliness and isolation, but through therapy, you can connect with others who share similar experiences. Group therapy or support groups offer a sense of community and understanding, helping you feel less alone in your struggle. Sharing your thoughts and feelings with individuals who genuinely empathize can provide immense comfort and encouragement.

Furthermore, therapy and counseling equip you with valuable tools to manage and cope with depression during the holiday season and beyond. Techniques such as cognitive-behavioral therapy (CBT) can help you challenge negative thoughts and reframe them in a more positive light. Through therapy, you can develop healthy coping mechanisms and learn effective stress-management techniques, allowing you to navigate the holiday season with resilience and self-compassion.

The benefits of therapy and counseling for individuals experiencing depression during the holiday season are immense. By seeking professional help, you can gain a deeper understanding of your emotions, develop effective coping strategies, build a support system, and practice self-care. Remember, you do not have to face this challenging time alone. Therapy and counseling can provide you with the guidance and support you need to embrace your emotions and find peace amidst the chaos.

Medication Management for Holiday Depression

The holiday season can be especially difficult for those of us experiencing depression. The joy often falls short and the need to celebrate and be together is often lacking. It can be especially difficult when everyone around you seems to be filled with happiness and excitement, further emphasizing the pressure to feel the same way. If you find yourself in this situation, it is important to remember that you are not alone, and there are strategies, including medication management, that can help you navigate this difficult period.

Medication can play a crucial role in managing holiday depression, alongside other therapeutic interventions. It is essential to consult with a healthcare professional who can assess your specific needs and provide appropriate guidance.

Medication for depression typically falls into two categories: antidepressants and anti-anxiety medications.

Antidepressants are commonly prescribed to help alleviate symptoms of depression. They work by balancing the levels of neurotransmitters in the brain, which can help regulate mood and improve overall well-being. It is important to note that antidepressants can take time to reach their full effect, so it is essential to start taking them early in the holiday season if needed. Additionally, finding the right medication and dosage may require some trial and error, as everyone's response to medication is unique. Regular communication with your healthcare provider is crucial to ensure the medication is working effectively and to address any potential side effects.

Anti-anxiety medications may also be prescribed to manage symptoms of depression during the holiday season. These medications can provide relief from anxiety, restlessness, and feelings of unease. However, they should be used cautiously and for short-term relief, as they may carry the risk of dependence or addiction. Your healthcare provider will carefully evaluate your symptoms and determine if anti-anxiety medication is appropriate for you.

It is important to remember that medication alone may not be sufficient to address holiday depression. In conjunction with medication management, engaging in therapy and self-care practices can greatly enhance your overall well-being. Therapy can provide a safe space to explore your emotions, develop coping strategies, and gain support from a mental health professional. Additionally, incorporating self-care activities such as exercise, mindfulness, and spending time with loved ones can help alleviate stress and improve your mood.

<u>PLEASE REMEMBER</u>: If your healthcare professional prescribes you medication to alleviate your symptoms, it is **CRUCIAL** that you take the medication as directed and that you do not stop taking the medication unless directed by your healthcare professional.

Remember, it is okay to not feel happy during the holiday season. Your emotions are valid, and seeking help is a brave and essential step towards healing. By embracing medication management and utilizing other therapeutic interventions, you can navigate the pressures of the holiday season while prioritizing your mental health. Reach out to your healthcare provider today and take the first step towards embracing your emotions in the holiday season.

Connecting with Support Groups and Online Communities

The holiday season is often portrayed as a time of joy, love, and celebration. However, for many people, especially those experiencing depression, it can be a challenging and emotionally draining time. While everyone around you seems to be caught up in the holiday spirit, you may find yourself feeling isolated, misunderstood, and overwhelmed. It's important to remember that you are not alone in your struggle, and there are support groups and online communities that can offer comfort, understanding, and a sense of belonging during this difficult period.

Support groups provide a safe space where individuals with similar experiences can come together to share their stories, offer support, and provide guidance. These groups are often led by trained professionals or individuals who have overcome depression during the holidays themselves. Being part of a support group can help you feel less alone and provide a sense of validation for your emotions. Hearing others' stories and coping strategies can also provide you with new perspectives and tools to navigate the holiday season.

In addition to in-person support groups, online communities have become a valuable resource for individuals facing depression during the holidays. These communities offer an accessible platform where you can connect with others from the comfort of your own home. They provide a space for discussion, sharing of experiences, and seeking advice from people who truly understand what you are going through. Online communities can be particularly beneficial for those who may feel uncomfortable or anxious about attending in-person meetings. They offer a sense of anonymity and allow you to engage at your own pace.

When seeking out support groups or online communities, it's important to find ones that align with your specific needs and interests. Look for groups that focus specifically on depression during the holidays or mental health support during this time. By connecting with individuals who share similar experiences, you can gain valuable insights, coping mechanisms, and a sense of camaraderie.

Remember, reaching out for support is not a sign of weakness but a courageous step towards healing. Connecting with support groups and online communities can offer you a sense of belonging, validation, and guidance during the holiday season. You don't have to face this challenging time alone – together, we can navigate the maze of holiday expectations and find solace in the understanding of others who truly comprehend the complexities of depression during this time.

If It's the Most Wonderful Time of the Year, Why Do I Feel Sad?!?

Chapter 9:

Moving Forward and Embracing Hope

Chapter 9: Moving Forward and Embracing Hope

Embracing the Journey of Healing and Recovery

The holiday season is often portrayed as a time of joy, love, and celebration. However, for many individuals, it can be a challenging and emotionally draining period, particularly for those who are experiencing depression. While society expects everyone to be happy and in high spirits during this time, it is essential to acknowledge and address the pressure that comes with this expectation.

Next, we will explore the importance of embracing the journey of healing and recovery during the holiday season. It is crucial to remember that healing is not linear, and it requires patience, self-compassion, and understanding. By recognizing and accepting your emotions, you can begin to navigate the holiday season in a way that feels authentic and true to yourself.

First and foremost, it is essential to acknowledge that it is okay not to feel happy during the holidays. Society often places unrealistic expectations on individuals, creating a facade that everyone should be joyful and merry. However, it is crucial to remind yourself that your emotions are valid and that it is okay to feel the way you do.

During this journey of healing and recovery, it is essential to prioritize self-care. This may involve setting boundaries with family and friends, taking time for yourself, and engaging in activities that bring you comfort and joy. It is essential to listen to your body and mind and give yourself permission to step away from festivities if they become overwhelming.

Additionally, seeking support from loved ones, therapists, or support groups can be incredibly beneficial during this time. Surrounding yourself with understanding and empathetic individuals can provide a sense of comfort and validation. Remember, you are not alone in your struggles, and reaching out for help is a sign of strength.

Lastly, it is essential to remind yourself that healing and recovery take time. The holiday season may act as a trigger for your depression, but it can also be an opportunity for growth and self-reflection. Embrace this journey and trust that you are moving towards a place of healing and recovery, even if it may not feel like it at times.

Addressing the pressure to be happy during the holiday season while experiencing depression can be overwhelming. However, by embracing the journey of healing and recovery, practicing self-care, seeking support, and allowing yourself to experience and express your emotions, you can navigate this time with greater authenticity and self-compassion. Remember, healing comes in its own time, and it is okay not to be okay during the holidays.

Celebrating Small Victories and Progress

The holiday season is often depicted as a time of joy, happiness, and celebration. We are bombarded with images of families coming together, laughter, and merriment. However, for those struggling with depression, this time of year can be incredibly challenging. The pressure to be happy when you are feeling down can feel overwhelming. It is important to recognize that your emotions are valid, and it is okay to not feel festive during the holidays.

Let's explore the significance of celebrating small victories and progress amidst the holiday season. While it may seem like everyone around you is radiating happiness, it is essential to remember that your journey is unique. Instead of comparing yourself to others, focus on your personal growth and accomplishments, no matter how small they may seem.

One way to acknowledge your progress is by setting realistic goals for yourself. Whether it is getting out of bed, engaging in self-care activities, or reaching out to a loved one for support, every step forward is worth celebrating. Recognize that even the smallest efforts can make a difference in your mental well-being. Embrace the fact that you are taking active steps towards healing and managing your depression, regardless of the time of year.

Another strategy to celebrate small victories is practicing gratitude. While it may be challenging to find joy in the midst of depression, try to identify at least one thing each day that you are grateful for. It could be as simple as a warm cup of tea, the sound of rain, or the comforting presence of a pet. Cultivating an attitude of gratitude can help shift your focus from the negativity that often accompanies depression, allowing you to find moments of solace and appreciation.

Additionally, it is crucial to surround yourself with a supportive network of friends or family who understand your struggles. Reach out to those who genuinely care about your well-being and can provide a listening ear or a comforting presence. Sharing your journey with empathetic individuals can help alleviate the feeling of isolation that often accompanies depression during the holiday season.

Remember, celebrating small victories and progress is not about conforming to societal expectations of happiness. It is about recognizing and honoring your own journey, no matter how difficult it may be. By acknowledging your efforts and achievements, you are empowering to continue moving forward, even when the holiday season feels overwhelming.

We must emphasize the importance of celebrating small victories and progress while addressing the pressure to be happy during the holiday season while experiencing depression. By setting realistic goals, practicing gratitude, and surrounding yourself with a supportive network, you can find solace and validation in your personal growth. Remember, you are not alone, and it is okay to prioritize your mental well-being above societal expectations. Celebrate your journey and take pride in each step forward, no matter how small.

Cultivating Hope for Future Holiday Seasons

It is important to explore practical strategies for addressing the pressure to be happy during the holiday season, while experiencing depression. By cultivating hope and focusing on self-care, we can navigate through these challenging times and look forward to brighter holiday seasons in the future.

1. **Recognizing and Accepting Your Emotions**: The first step towards cultivating hope is acknowledging and accepting your feelings of depression during the holidays. Understand that it is okay to feel sad or low, even when societal expectations dictate otherwise. Give yourself permission to experience your emotions without judgment or guilt.

2. **Setting Realistic Expectations**: It's crucial to set realistic expectations for yourself during the holiday season. Understand that you may not feel as joyful or energetic as others, and that's perfectly fine. Focus on what you are capable of doing and be gentle with yourself. Don't compare your experience to others; remember that everyone's journey is unique.

3. **Seeking Support**: Reach out to trusted friends, family, or mental health professionals who can provide support during this challenging time. Surrounding yourself with compassionate individuals who understand your situation can offer solace and comfort. Consider joining support groups or online communities where you can connect with others facing similar struggles.

4. **Practicing Self-Care**: Make self-care a priority during the holiday season. Engage in activities that bring you joy, whether it's reading a book, taking a walk in nature, or practicing meditation. Prioritize your mental and physical well-being by maintaining a regular sleep schedule, eating nutritious meals, and exercising regularly.

5. **Creating New Traditions**: If traditional holiday activities trigger negative emotions, consider creating new traditions that align with your current emotional state. Focus on activities that bring you peace and comfort, such as volunteering, engaging in creative endeavors, or spending quality time with loved ones in a low-pressure environment.

Remember that it is possible to cultivate hope for future holiday seasons despite experiencing depression. By acknowledging and accepting your emotions, setting realistic expectations, seeking support, practicing self-care, and creating new traditions, you can navigate through the holiday season with greater ease. Embrace the healing journey and know that brighter days lie ahead.

Chapter 10:

Spreading Awareness and Advocacy

If It's the Most Wonderful Time of the Year, Why Do I Feel Sad?!?

If It's the Most Wonderful Time of the Year, Why Do I Feel Sad?!?

Chapter 10: Spreading Awareness and Advocacy

Sharing Personal Stories and Experiences

In a world that often expects us to be cheerful and full of joy during the holiday season, it can be incredibly challenging for those who are silently battling depression. While everyone around you seems to be reveling in the festivities, you may find yourself feeling isolated, misunderstood, and even more depressed. But, dear reader, know that you are not alone in this struggle.

Let's visit the pressure society places on individuals to be happy during the holiday season, while acknowledging and embracing the experiences of those who are dealing with depression. It is important to remember that your emotions and experiences are valid, even if they do not align with the societal expectations of holiday cheer.

One powerful way to combat the loneliness and isolation you may feel with others, is by opening up and connecting with individuals who have faced similar challenges, you can find solace and understanding, by sharing your personal stories.

Sharing personal stories and experiences is a powerful way to break down the barriers of isolation and stigma. It provides a platform for individuals to express their truth, fostering empathy and understanding within the community.

Let us share our stories, embrace our emotions, and support one another through the holiday season and beyond. By doing so, we can create a world that acknowledges and celebrates the diversity of human experiences, even during a time that seems to demand endless cheer.

Supporting Mental Health Initiatives during the Holidays

It is crucial to acknowledge that depression does not discriminate, and it can affect anyone, regardless of the time of year. However, during the holidays, there is an added layer of societal pressure to be happy and engaged in the festivities. It is important to remember that your feelings are valid, and it is okay to not feel joyful during this time. It is crucial to prioritize self-care and recognize that it is okay to take a step back from the expectations and obligations that come with the holiday season.

One way to support mental health initiatives during the holidays is by cultivating a support system. Reach out to trusted friends or family members who can provide a listening ear and understanding. It can be helpful to express your emotions and concerns, knowing that you are not alone in your experience. Additionally, consider seeking professional help from therapists or support groups specializing in mental health during the holidays. These resources can provide guidance and strategies to cope with depression specifically during this time of year.

Another important aspect of supporting mental health initiatives during the holidays is setting boundaries. It is okay to decline invitations or limit your participation in events that may exacerbate your depression. Give yourself permission to prioritize your mental well-being and engage in activities that bring you comfort and joy, even if they are non-traditional holiday activities. Remember, there is no right or wrong way to experience the holiday season.

Lastly, practicing self-compassion is crucial. Be patient with yourself and allow yourself to feel your emotions without judgment. Understand that it is okay to have both good and bad days, and that healing takes time. Surround yourself with positive affirmations and engage in self-care practices that resonate with you, such as meditation, exercise, or creative outlets.

Addressing the pressure to be happy during the holiday season while experiencing depression is vital for supporting mental health initiatives. By cultivating a support system, setting boundaries, and practicing self-compassion, individuals can navigate this challenging time with greater ease. Remember, your mental health is a priority, and it is okay to prioritize yourself during the holiday season.

Inspiring Others to Embrace Their Emotions and Seek Help

In a society that expects joy and happiness during the holiday season, it can be incredibly challenging for those who are experiencing depression. The pressure to put on a smiling facade while battling inner turmoil can be overwhelming. However, it is essential to remember that you are not alone in this struggle. My hope is to inspire individuals who are depressed during the holidays to embrace their emotions and seek the help they need, while addressing the societal pressure to be happy.

Remember, it's okay not to be okay during the holiday season. Embrace your emotions, challenge societal expectations, seek help, and prioritize self-care. By doing so, you are taking steps towards reclaiming your well-being and finding solace in the midst of a holiday season that may not always live up to the hype. Let this be a time of self-discovery, growth, and healing – a season where you learn to embrace your emotions and find hope for a brighter future.

If It's the Most Wonderful Time of the Year, Why Do I Feel Sad?!?

If It's the Most Wonderful Time of the Year, Why Do I Feel Sad?!?

If It's the Most Wonderful Time of the Year, Why Do I Feel Sad?!?

Chapter 11:

In Conclusion...

If It's the Most Wonderful Time of the Year, Why Do I Feel Sad?!?

If It's the Most Wonderful Time of the Year, Why Do I Feel Sad?!?

Conclusion: Embracing Your Emotions for a More Authentic Holiday Experience

In this book, "If It's the Most Wonderful Time of the Year, Why Am I So Sad?!?" we have explored the pressure to be happy during the holidays, particularly when one is experiencing depression. We have discussed the façade that society often expects us to put on, hiding our true emotions behind smiles and forced cheer. However, we have also emphasized the importance of embracing and accepting our emotions, as they are a natural part of the human experience.

While it may be challenging to embrace your emotions during the holiday season, doing so can lead to a more authentic and fulfilling experience. By acknowledging and accepting your feelings of depression, you can begin to navigate the holiday season with a greater sense of self-compassion and understanding. It is okay to not feel happy all the time, and it is okay to prioritize your mental health during this time of year.

Rather than forcing yourself to conform to societal expectations, consider creating your own meaningful holiday traditions that align with your authentic self. This could involve spending time alone, seeking support from loved ones, or engaging in activities that bring you comfort and solace. Remember, the holiday season is about finding joy and meaning in your own way, not about meeting others' expectations.

It is crucial to embrace your emotions during the holiday season, even if they are not the expected feelings of happiness. By acknowledging and accepting your depression, you can navigate this time of year with greater authenticity and self-compassion. Remember, your emotions are valid, and it is okay to prioritize your mental health above all else. By doing so, you can create a more authentic and fulfilling holiday experience for yourself, regardless of societal pressures.

As the final pages draw near, let us embrace the essence of self-love and the importance of caring for ourselves during the holiday season. It is time to bid farewell to all the chaos and stress that may have weighed us down, and welcome the joy and peace that lie on the horizon.

The holiday season, with all its festivities and obligations, can sometimes become overwhelming. But armed with the knowledge we have gained, we can navigate this time with grace and tenderness towards ourselves. We have learned that it is not selfish to prioritize our own needs; in fact, it is essential for our overall happiness and fulfillment.

As the holiday lights twinkle and the air fills with laughter and cheer, let us not lose sight of the love we owe ourselves. Let us make a pledge to prioritize self-love, not just during the holidays but every day of the year. This commitment will allow us to shine brighter, love deeper, and embrace the joy that life has to offer.

And so, dear reader, as we reach the end, let us carry the lessons of self-love and care with us. May we revel in the warmth of our own hearts, finding solace and peace within ourselves. As we bid adieu to this narrative, let it be a reminder that loving and taking care of ourselves is not just a seasonal endeavor but a lifelong journey.

May you embrace the holidays and every day that follows with a newfound appreciation for the beautiful soul that you are. Remember, you are worthy of love, happiness, and the utmost care. So, go forth and end this holiday season as best as you can, knowing that you have the power to create a life filled with self-love and abundant joy.

I LOVE YOU FOR BEING HERE- *M*

I pledge to love and take care of myself during the holidays and every day, setting healthy boundaries and making myself the priority.

X______________________________________

If It's the Most Wonderful Time of the Year, Why Do I Feel Sad?!?

If It's the Most Wonderful Time of the Year, Why Do I Feel Sad?!?